The Go-Getter Mentality

How to Be Proactive in Life to Ensure Your Own Success

by Preena Bhardwaj

Table of Contents

Introduction 1

Chapter 1: Developing Self-Awareness 7

Chapter 2: The Art of Goal Setting 13

Chapter 3: Taking Action and Moving Forward 19

Chapter 4: Fighting the Pitfalls of the Go Getter Mentality 27

Chapter 5: Playing Fair 33

Conclusion 37

Introduction

While there are arguably countless factors that contribute to success, the only way to guarantee success is by taking action. Intellect, talent, opportunity, and resources will never amount to anything unless you do something with them.

The idea of success is quite relative; people achieve it in various gradients. Some people achieve it quite early in their life, while others achieve it later on. Some rarely achieve it while others achieve it quite frequently. Finally, some people arrive at success because they are lucky, while others get there with a bit of hard work and grit.

Ideally, those who aim for success should do so with certainty. These are the kind of people who, as the old saying goes, "make their own luck." By doing so, they get an edge over everybody else.

Making your own luck is what being proactive or a "go getter" is all about. As opposed to simply being active and engaged, being proactive means leading a lifestyle where every opportunity is seized, every problem is resolved without delay, and no task is ever put off until tomorrow.

For example, an active person is one that participates or engages in a lot of activities but may choose to take advantage of one opportunity but not the next one. A go getter, on the other hand, will take advantage of every opportunity that comes their way, even when he or she has a choice.

Go getters never choose to slow down when they can take the dive nor will they ever leave anything to chance. They will do everything in their power to achieve their goals, both short term and long term. And yes, they have a very clear vision of what their goals are.

This, of course, is easier said than done. Like most things in life, you have to work harder if you want to get ahead of others. Most people who aren't proactive are where they are now not because they don't want to be better or do better, but because they don't know how to be better or they don't realize that they can be better.

This is exactly what this guide is for. Here, we'll take a look at the things that make a person closer to the ideal active lifestyle. You will learn how to condition yourself in all aspects of your life - even those aspects you thought didn't matter, but actually do - so that you'll always be making your own luck.

In short, this guide will help you learn how to be a go getter.

© Copyright 2014 by Miafn LLC - All rights reserved.

This document is geared towards providing reliable information in regards to the topic and issue covered. The publication is sold with the idea that the publisher is not required to render accounting, officially permitted, or otherwise, qualified services. If advice is necessary, legal or professional, a practiced individual in the profession should be ordered.

- From a Declaration of Principles which was accepted and approved equally by a Committee of the American Bar Association and a Committee of Publishers and Associations.

In no way is it legal to reproduce, duplicate, or transmit any part of this document in either electronic means or in printed format. Recording of this publication is strictly prohibited and any storage of this document is not allowed unless with written permission from the publisher. All rights reserved.

The information provided herein is stated to be truthful and consistent, in that any liability, in terms of inattention or otherwise, by any usage or abuse of any policies, processes, or directions contained within is solely and completely the responsibility of the recipient reader. Under no circumstances will any legal responsibility or blame be held against the publisher for any reparation, damages, or monetary loss due to the information herein, either directly or indirectly.

Respective authors own all copyrights not held by the publisher.

The information herein is offered for informational purposes solely, and is universal as so. The presentation of the information is without contract or any type of guarantee assurance.

The trademarks that are used are without any consent, and the publication of the trademark is without permission or backing by the trademark owner. All trademarks and brands within this book are for clarifying purposes only and are the owned by the owners themselves, not affiliated with this document.

Chapter 1: Developing Self-Awareness

Because the go getter mentality is a state of mind, it's important to first be familiar with it, as in, to know what it means to have that particular mentality. This includes:

- Knowing what the mentality is;
- Knowing what the mentality is NOT; and
- Identifying the indicators of having that mentality.

Once you become familiar with this concept, you will be able to gauge whether or not you already have this mentality. If you already have this mentality (good for you!), the concepts will allow you to know if there's anything you can do to get better at it. And of course, if you find that you don't have this mentality, then this should definitely be your first step to becoming a go getter.

The Mentality IS:

Goal Oriented. Being proactive doesn't mean being hyperactive. Go getters do something because there's a purpose behind it, and not just because they can do it. Otherwise, what's the point? If getting or doing something doesn't have a point, then you're just wasting your time.

Spontaneous. This might seem like an exact opposite of being detailed or goal oriented, but when life does not turn out the way it was expected, a proactive person knows how to wing it. Spontaneous people have goals and are aware of the details, but they know how to change their actions to adapt to the unpredictable life events.

Detailed. Proactive people not only know what they want, they have a crystal clear picture of it. This is important for setting short and long terms goals, and for assessing them at regular intervals.

Patient. Success takes time, and being proactive not only about taking action at the right time but it is also about taking action in general. When doing something sooner than later defeats your purpose, it is better to be patient and wait.

Self-Assessing. Even successful people experience failure at some point in their lives. What helps them succeed is that they take time to acknowledge what they've done so far, realize where they went wrong, and learn from their mistakes.

The Mentality IS NOT:

Random. Doing something for no reason at all is, by definition, what wasting time is all about. Doing things just for the sake of doing it will always come at a cost of not being able to do something that is more productive. Some people randomly do things during the day to feel productive, but this, in fact, is a fake kind of productivity since it's got nothing to do with their set goals; if they have any in the first place.

Obsessive Compulsive. Proactive people do NOT break down or lose their temper when things don't go according to plan. On the contrary, it takes a lot of flexibility and composure to work through an unexpected turn of events as doing so actually reaps greater benefits.

Vague. Let's illustrate. Imagine that you want to buy a bag, which you will use while traveling. One detail you need to figure out is how much stuff you're going to carry. If you don't, you might end up getting a bag that can't accommodate everything you need. Needless to say, this is set a lot of terrible setbacks to your trip. Go getters will never make this mistake because they know how to plan the details of their journey towards their goals well ahead of the actual journey.

Lazy or Impulsive. These are people are those who either procrastinate, thinking they've got all the time in the world, or those who are incredibly impatient, demanding things right now like there's no tomorrow. On the flip side, proactive people believe there is a right time for everything.

Incorrigible. These are the people who think that they are never wrong, blame others, and never take responsibility for their actions. If your plan is to ensure your own success, you need to take full responsibility for everything that's within your control. Otherwise, you leave your success to chance and you have no actual control over it.

Do I Have the Go Getter Mentality?

People who don't have goals in life probably wouldn't be reading this at all. So if you're reading this guide, hoping to achieve certain goals, there's a big chance that you do have the go getter mentality. Try asking yourself these questions:

Note: When answering these questions, try imagining a number of specific instances that can help you answer these questions and try to compare how you fared in each instance. The more recent the experience, the better – that way it's much more vivid.

- Am I getting things done on time?
- Do I save on time, money, and effort when working towards reaching my goals?
- Do the people I work or deal with end up liking me more after working with me?
- Do I feel like I am progressing? Am I faced with more opportunities as I go on?
- Am I open to criticism, thinking that they help me become better?
- When something goes wrong, do I feel less guilty knowing that I did my best?

If you answered "yes" to all of these questions, then you're probably one of the best go getters there are. The advice in this guide will help you perfect your craft from a different perspective.

If you answered "yes" to most of these questions, then you're a go getter in your own respect. Now all you have to do is to improve what you've been doing so far, and this guide can help you do that.

If you answered "no" to most of these questions, then there's still a lot for you to work on. But consider yourself lucky, because this guide might just be what you need to get there.

Chapter 2: The Art of Goal Setting

It cannot be stressed enough: You have to know what you want. Having no goals is the biggest waste of time there is. So this is where you should start.

Visualize!

Remember that old advice which says to "visualize yourself at the end"? That advice is not just old; it's gold! Instead of going right ahead and working on something, take some time off before you begin to just imagine what the end result of your plans will look like. Think about the times you've achieved your goals by thinking about the following:

- What you've accomplished
- Where you're standing
- Who you're with
- How you feel

The more vivid your visualization, the better it is. Visualizations are the pictures in your mind and when you have a clear image in your head of everything you plan to do and where you plan to end up, you've already won half the battle.

Besides, it's more fun imagining yourself being successful. Enjoy a little bit of that before you start working hard.

Details, Details

Again, the more vivid the image in your mind is the better. It's always better to be specific because details make your goals realistic and anything short of a realistic goal is never healthy as they usually result to frustration.

Imagine a friend walking up to you and saying "I want to be rich." Come on, who doesn't want to be? But the thing about being rich is that it's very relative. There's never a specific income bracket for being rich.

But assume for the moment, for the purposes of this example, that your goal is to be rich. What does being "rich" mean to you? That's where the details come in. Take these questions to begin with:

- How much do you want to earn in a year?
- What would be the source of these earnings?
- Is how much would you want to earn and have to pay for relative to these earnings?

If, for example, your idea of being rich is being able to buy the simple stuff you need without having to stress yourself out over a 24/7 desk job, and still have time for your family, then that's a much better goal than simply being rich. Why? Because of the details of the goal.

Also, a detailed goal makes it easier to assess whether something is realistic in your situation or not. This will be great for setting short and long term goals.

Note: On Goals and Ideas

In a nutshell, goals are more specific than ideas. Saying that you want to be rich is merely an idea, but stating how much you want to earn from a specific job each year is a more vivid goal.

Don't confuse one for the other!

The Most Important Detail: When?

If you don't know when you want to achieve your goal, chances are the answer is never. You have to know exactly when you expect yourself to make it big. Taking from the "being rich" goal, you'll want to know approximately when you'll get your next raise or promotion and, ultimately, when you have accomplished all your goals.

Deadlines are great for benchmarking your progress. They tell you how far you have come and how much further you have left before you get there. You get to tell yourself: "I should have achieved (insert goal) by now."

Take on a Proactive Goal

Set goals that require you to take action or achieve something rather than those that push you to avoid or prevent you from doing something. The latter is just being negative.

Take kids for example. When you tell them not to do something, they most likely end up doing it. The same thing goes on in your brain. What if someone tells you to not think of an elephant? That's right: the image of an elephant appears in your mind.

In short, keep things positive. If you're about to perform in front of a live audience and you keep telling yourself that the crowd is going to love you, you'll most likely end up performing better than if you were telling yourself not to mess up.

Some people call this the Law of Attraction (i.e. making things happen by actively or subliminally thinking about it). Whatever you wish to call it, just stay positive!

On a more practical note, being positive does seem like the more logical thing to do. After all, how do you go about not doing something? It's better to focus on what needs to be done and doing it rather than not doing it.

Chapter 3: Taking Action and Moving Forward

The best plans are always easier said than done. But as long as your goals are clear and realistic, you'll be able to inch or leap your way to them, no matter what obstacles come your way.

Be Prepared: Make Plans!

While being spontaneous is one of the go getter's most powerful tools (we'll get to that a little later), it's obviously much better if you make your own plans. After all, that's what making your own luck is all about.

This is actually your first step to taking action. This includes:

- Getting enough information about the task that you have to do
- Preparing all the stuff you need to get the task done
- Knowing who or what you'll be working with
- Building a routine

The Power of Asking Questions

Nobody has all the answers, and the best way to figure things out is to ask. However, many people are scared to do that. It's ridiculous how some people are too scared to ask an employee at the office where they can find someone, or ask the sales person which items are on sale. In the end, they waste a lot of time or miss out on many opportunities.

It's probably because they're afraid they will be rejected or they don't want people to think they don't know something.

If this is a habit of yours, get rid of it! Stop trying to think that you know the answer to everything because a know-it-all gets nowhere. Admit it to yourself that you've still got a long way to go and surround yourself with people who can teach you a thing or two about getting where you want to go.

The rule of thumb is this: if there's no sign that says asking questions is prohibited, then go ahead and ask! People won't bite you for asking questions (at least the sane ones won't). Worst case scenario, they ignore you. When that happens, just go look for someone else. Whatever shame you feel on admitting that you don't know something will never outweigh the embarrassment of failing because you had no idea what you were doing.

Note: Don't forget to ask nicely. It does wonders!

Stop Comparing and Work With What You Have

Some people give up easily because they feel like they don't have the means to accomplish their goals. This usually comes from comparing yourself with other people who are in a better position than you.

You've obviously met someone who felt discouraged entering a competition or taking the lead in a project because he or she thinks there is someone else who has more experience or who has better materials than them.

It's never healthy to compare yourself with others because in the real world, there will always be some people who are ahead of you, but there will also be some people who are always behind you. That's life. But what anybody can do is work their way up.

Think of it this way: that person you envy so much for having a college degree or having more money for capital didn't get all that by just sitting around. At some point, they did something to get where they are now, and so can you.

Consider what you need, what you have, and what else you need to get to achieve your goals. Do you need to secure some documents to get that job position? Do you need a team to start your small business? Some things are harder to get than others, but one thing's for sure: you're not going to get them by just sitting around and looking at someone else.

Tip: Instead of just envying that guy with the big business, why not go ahead and ask him for advice?

Work with People. Make Friends!
Everything in life cannot be done alone. Even the smallest business plan requires a group of specialists. So unless you're an accountant, a marketing agent, and a human resource

person all in one, you'll need help. To move forward, you will have to accept that you can't do everything.

If you're not working with a team already (i.e. freelancing), you will have to work with other people sometime or another. Go getters need to know how to get together with the right people to get the work done.

How do you do that?

- Be nice. Make people your friends. Don't make them feel like you're only working with them because you have to. Nobody wants to feel like they're being used. Tip: Make sure you always remember their names!

- Consider other people's needs. If you're contracting people's services, make sure you are fair to them in every way. Taking too much from anything at any point in your endeavor will cause you to lose more than what you will gain out of it.

In short, be nice. Motivate people so that they want to work with you more and they will help you move forward. That's how a go getter gets people to work with him or her.

Note: Remember that even making friends and being part of social groups or extra-curricular activities can be goals too! Apply these principles anywhere you work and interact with people. Go getters excel in all aspects of life, not just business.

Make a Habit of Doing it, Now!

Procrastination is the dark horse that can ruin anyone's career. People know it's there but we don't pay it any heed. Next thing you know, hours or even days have gone by. So much time is wasted when you procrastinate!

Listen to the old advice: don't put off for tomorrow what you can do today. Postponing tasks can develop into a terrible habit that affects everything you want to get done.

The key to beating this terrible roadblock lies in proper discipline and goal setting.

- **Use those deadlines!** It's amazing how your body can get that burst of energy when deadlines are close. If you're the kind of person that crams, then make the most of this by baiting it with deadlines.

    Deadlines can be tricky when they're self-imposed though (we tend to go easy on ourselves). But if you're well aware of the consequences of missing a deadline, then it'll feel like someone else is demanding that you finish the job on time.

- **Set alarms and limits.** These are for those things that don't involve work. Make sure your breaks, meals, and even baths are regulated. This might not seem much, but this will actually helping you form a habit of doing things within a specific time frame. At the very least, it doesn't give your mind and body the chance to think that it's okay to take your time when you should do otherwise.

Try to keep a mental note in your head of how well you're doing with every step. Feeling good about what you're doing is part of the go getter mentality. We tend to master tasks that we enjoy more. So when you do something right, compliment yourself for it and keep up the good work.

Chapter 4: Fighting the Pitfalls of the Go Getter Mentality

Mastering the go getter mentality can be a hit and miss sometimes. It requires experience. These pitfalls happen when you forget what the go getter mentality is. But more than knowing how to avoid these mistakes, you also need to know how to move on after the inevitable happens.

Contingencies: Hope for the Best and Prepare for the Worst

Most things in life never go according to plan. What you visualize in the beginning will always be, at best, an ideal situation or outcome. If things turn out as you expected, then good! But sometimes deadlines are not met, clients back out, business partners change their minds, and unexpected things happen. Here are some tips for dealing with the unexpected:

1. **Prepare for them.** This comes with experience. As time goes by, you'll know what can go wrong with your business, your work, or whatever project you are endeavoring to complete. Go getters don't wait to look for solutions when the problems are there already. They create a series of plan B's and C's well in advance just in case they're needed.

   Do the people you work with usually come late? Is it likely to rain? What problems have you faced in the past?

While it may be true that spontaneity can be a blessing, it's equally important to keep in mind that luck will always favor the prepared.

2. **Stop Pointing Fingers.** You won't get anything out of it. Instead, keep your eye on the goal and work with what you have. Things may have gone bad, but remember that blaming others, or refusing to take responsibility, will achieve nothing, and at most will make matters worse.

3. **Evaluate Your Options.** If you have time, take a deep breath and consider the things that you can do. Is there someone you can call? Do you have an alternative plan? What can you do to make up for the lapse in judgment?

4. **Take Notes.** The worst thing you can do when you make a mistake is to not learn from it. Always analyze why something happens and see what can be done to avoid making the same mistake again in the future. This is how you make it easier to do item #1.

Note: Dealing with others who made mistakes. This is important especially when you're working with other people. While it's not healthy to take your frustration out on the people responsible, it is important to debrief them about what happened as much as it is to go over it with yourself.

Proactive people already have an advantage when it comes to asserting their authority over their co-workers or teammates simply because they've already set a good example by helping others deal with the problem.

Try to tell them what they did right and focus on what they can improve on while gently discussing what they did wrong. Go getters will make sure not to put other people on the defensive so that they're more open to criticisms.

Getting Complaints: Learning to Take Criticisms

Remember that a go getter never pretends to know everything. Part of this trait is knowing how to accept not only their mistakes, but to also welcome criticism from others. While this is especially important when taking pointers on improvement from mentors or superiors, you should also learn to accept comments from peers and other people as well.

While you're not expected to follow everyone's advice, accepting the comments of as many people as you can will widen your options prior to deciding what to improve on.

Plus, humility goes a long way in this competitive world. You're better off accepting the complaints of others with grace rather than building a reputation of being unapproachable by others.

Ultimately, go getters are really good at focusing on what to improve on, and they get a lot out of the criticism that they get, and not the praises.

Proper Timing: Be Patient

Success requires sacrifice. Sometimes you have to give your endeavors time to grow. No business or plan has ever borne fruits overnight.

On the one hand, we know it's important to not procrastinate. It's important to always do something today instead of putting it off for tomorrow. On the other hand, it's also important not to rush into things until you've prepared for them. Sometimes we get too worked up by an opportunity that we forget to think twice about it. Many people are really good at hoodwinking people that they can take advantage of. Don't be their victim!

Always think twice before investing a huge sum of money in a business venture. Ask if people around you are okay with your plan. Before finally leaving to catch a flight, double check to make sure you've got everything you need packed in your bags.

Don't rush into things. You might regret it.

Consider All the Consequences of Your Decision

Imagine buying a house. Some people will set their goal as expanding their home or getting a new house, but they don't weigh in all the other factors involved, such as the increase in taxes, maintenance fees, and even the insurance policy value. By the time people realize that the cons outweigh the pros of their decisions, it's already too late.

Go getters are also always mindful of how their decisions will affect other people.

As mentioned before, the go getter mentality is not an impulsive and impatient mentality. Go getters achieve their goals efficiently. They reach their goals with as many gains and as few losses as possible.

Chapter 5: Playing Fair

Finally, go getters need to know that the end never justifies the means. Sustaining a proactive life means playing by the rules. It cannot be stressed enough how much a person can be bitten in the butt by cutting corners somewhere in between.

- **Follow the Law.** If you're running a business, know what the legal requirements are, and apply for the licenses you need by following the proper procedures. Always pay your dues and comply with all the requirements. Don't put your life's work at risk simply because you were too lazy to follow the rules at some point. It's also your responsibility to know what lawful regulations exist in the place where you are and abide by them.

- **Honor Agreements.** Don't forget that you never get to where you are alone. If you contracted the help of someone one way or another, make sure you pay or give the other party(s) what's due to them. Not only is breaching a contract against the law, it's also bad for your reputation, no matter what you are doing. If someone helps you out for free, make it a point to say thank you and try reciprocating their favor one way or another.

- **Be Honest.** Many successful businesses are built on trust. Break that foundation and you lose your chance of maximizing your potential. A person with a proactive or go getter mentality is bound to be well known, so misrepresenting yourself either directly or through others is never a good idea. People appreciate honesty in the long run.

Conclusion

Finally, take note that being a go getter is all about practice. Don't expect to get things right the first time around (especially when forming those habits). Always keep in mind the following points:

- Be self-aware of your current mentality.
- Have clear goals. Know what you want.
- Visualize and set your goals properly.
- Always be prepared.
- Always aim to work now rather than later.
- Play fair. Keep everything legal.

Keep this list in your planner or pin it to your refrigerator door to keep reminding yourself of these tips. They may seem simple, but don't take them for granted at any time. You'd be surprised to know how many times these simple tips have been the secret of so many successful people.

Strive to have a proactive lifestyle by following the guide above and you'll eventually become better at it. Not only is being proactive a good way to ensure your success, but it's also your best bet at dealing with unexpected turns of events. You will always be the one in control. It's also great to be known as the proactive person who knows how to deal with others.

All these, and more, are what will ensure your own success.

Finally, I'd like to thank you for purchasing this book! If you enjoyed it or found it helpful, I'd greatly appreciate it if you'd take a moment to leave a review on Amazon. Thank you!

Printed in Great Britain
by Amazon